Transportation & Communication Series

Motorcycles

Dee Stuart

 Enslow Publishers, Inc.

40 Industrial Road	PO Box 38
Box 398	Aldershot
Berkeley Heights, NJ 07922	Hants GU12 6BP
USA	UK

http://www.enslow.com

For William James Reimer, Best Boy

The publisher wishes to thank Laura S. Jeffrey for her efforts in researching and editing this book.

Library of Congress Cataloging-in-Publication Data

Stuart, Dee.
    Motorcycles / Dee Stuart.
        p. cm. — (Transportation & communication series)
    Includes bibliographical references and index.
    ISBN 0-7660-1648-X
    1. Motorcycles—Juvenile literature. [1. Motorcycles.] I. Title. II.
    Series.
TL440.15 .S78 2001
629.227'5—dc21   00-011349

Printed in the United States of America

10 9 8 7 6 5 4 3 2 1

To Our Readers:
We have done our best to make sure all Internet addresses in this book were active and appropriate when we went to press. However, the author and the publisher have no control over and assume no liability for the material available on those Internet sites or on other Web sites they may link to. Any comments or suggestions can be sent by e-mail to comments@enslow.com or to the address on the back cover.

Illustration Credits: AP Photo/Matthew Cavanaugh, p.28 (top); AP Photo/Gael Cornier, p. 40; AP Photo/The Ledger, Paul Johnson, p. 43; AP Photo/Los Angeles Daily News, David Sprague, p. 42; Archive Photos, pp. 10, 12; Corel Corporation, pp. 4, 6, 20, 22 (bottom), 24, 25, 34, 37, 38, 39 (bottom); Denver Public Library, Western History Collection, pp. 23, 26; Express Newspapers/Archive Photos, pp. 9, 11, 13; Fotos International/Archive Photos, p. 8; Hemera Technologies, Inc. 1997–2000, pp. 1, 2, 5, 7, 15, 16, 21, 22 (top), 27, 35, 36, 39 (top), 41; Kristin McCarthy, pp. 17, 18; Courtesy of Motorcycle Hall of Fame Museum, pp. 14, 28 (bottom), 29, 31, 32; Pederson Collection, p. 33; Beth Townsend, p. 19; *The World*, p. 30.

Cover Illustration: Corel Corporation

Contents

Acknowledgments

Dee Stuart wishes to thank the following people for their assistance:

Don Brown, Motorcycle Industry Council

J. D. Dollins

Stephanie Gunn, Motorcycle Industry Council

Babs Lakey

Tom Lewis

Deborah Morris

Jeff Morrow

Sandy Steen

Lynn Stewart, Motorcycle Training Center (Richardson, Texas)

Chapter 1

A Daredevil Motorcycle Rider

Motorcycles are one of the most exciting ways to get around. Riders become part of the world they travel through. They feel the sun, wind, and rain. They smell the flowers and trees. They see things up close as they zip along country roads and highways.

Most people use motorcycles to get from one place to another. Some race motorcycles. Others use motorcycles to do stunts.

Some people like to race their motorcycles (left).

Robert Craig "Evel" Knievel is a famous motorcycle stuntman. In 1966, Evel Knievel began performing in motorcycle stunt shows. He rode through flaming tunnels and jumped over vehicles.

On New Year's Day in 1968, Knievel performed a dangerous stunt. He tried to jump across fountains in front of Caesar's Palace in Las Vegas, Nevada. The distance was 151

Evel Knievel soars over two vans during a practice jump.

feet! Evel cleared the fountains, but he crashed when he landed. He was badly hurt. Evel spent almost a month in the hospital.

Evel recovered from his injuries. He did many other shows. His stunts became more and more dangerous. In February 1971, Evel set a world record. He jumped over nineteen cars. But in May 1971, Evel crashed when he tried to jump over thirteen trucks. Ten months later, he crashed again during his next stunt. Once again, Evel was badly hurt. But he did not quit.

In February 1973, Evel used a ski-style ramp to jump over fifty cars in the Los Angeles Coliseum. The next year, he jumped over eight Mack trucks at the Canadian National Exposition. He earned a lot of money with his motorcycle stunts. Many of them were shown on television.

Evel Knievel flies over 13 double-decker buses in London, England, May 1975.

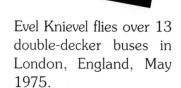

One day, Evel said that he would jump over the Grand Canyon in Arizona. Government officials told him he could not try this stunt. So Evel decided to jump over the Snake River Canyon instead. Evel added rockets to his motorcycle. He called it a "Skycycle." He also wore a parachute. If he did not make the jump, he would fall safely to the river below.

On September 8, 1974, Evel revved the

Evel points to his Skycycle. He used it in a stunt over Snake River Canyon.

engine of his Skycycle and began to fly. Instead of going across the canyon, Evel went down. He opened his parachute and floated to the ground. The stunt failed, but Evel kept performing. In May 1975, he jumped over thirteen double-decker buses at Wembley Stadium in London. In October 1975, he jumped over fourteen Greyhound buses at King's Island in Ohio.

Evel Knievel never lets crashes like this one stop him from jumping again.

Evel Knievel in front of the 14 buses he jumped over during a stunt in October 1975.

Then, in 1976, Evel tried to jump his motorcycle over a tank of live sharks. The stunt was shown on television. Millions of people watched as Evel jumped—and crashed. Evel broke both of his arms, and he hurt his head. A person watching also was injured. Evel decided it was time to stop. He taught his son Robbie how to perform motorcycle stunts.

Evel is called America's legendary daredevil.

His motorcycle is on display in the Smithsonian Institute's Museum of American History. Motorcycles made him rich and famous. But they cost Evel his health. During his career, Evel broke more than 35 bones. He spent a total of 36 months—that is three years—in the hospital. Evel's motorcycle stunts were awesome. But it would be wise not to try to copy them.

Evel Knievel always has time to greet his fans.

Chapter 2

How Motorcycles Work

Motorcycles look like bicycles. In fact, motorcycles often are called "bikes." People who ride motorcycles are called bikers. But a motorcycle is heavier than a bicycle. Also, a motorcycle has an engine. The engine is what makes the motorcycle go. Motorcycles can go as fast as cars. Some can go even faster!

Motorcycle engines have anywhere from one to six cylinders. The more cylinders an engine has, the more powerful it is. A cylinder is a round metal tube with a closed end. The closed end is called the head. Fuel and air enter the sealed cylinder. A piston inside the

Motorcycle engines (left) may look small, but they are powerful.

Spark plugs and chains are important parts of motorcycles.

cylinder moves up. It squeezes the fuel and air. Then, a spark from a plug causes an explosion inside the cylinder. The explosion makes power.

Other parts of a motorcycle are the transmission system, wheels, brakes, and controls. The transmission system sends power from the engine to the rear wheel. The rear wheel has a clutch, gearbox, and chain.

When the rider changes gears or stops, the clutch acts as a switch between the engine and the gearbox. The gearbox keeps the engine from quitting or going too fast. The chain goes from a small front sprocket to a large sprocket on the rear wheel. It turns the rear wheel to move the motorcycle.

Wheels come in three types. There are pressed steel wheels, spoke wheels, and mag wheels. Pressed steel wheels are the ones on most motorcycles. Spoke wheels are larger, stronger, and heavier than pressed steel wheels. Mag wheels are lighter and stronger than spoke wheels.

The wheels hold the tires. Some motorcycles need special tires. For example, motorcycles called dirt bikes are used for off-road travel. Tires on dirt bikes are narrower. They also have special bumps on them called nubs. Nubs help keep the tires from popping when they go over rocks and uneven places.

Motorcycles have six major controls. They make the motorcycle stop and go. These controls are the handlebars, throttle, front brake, rear brake, clutch, and shift. The handlebars control direction. The throttle controls speed. The brakes stop the motorcycle. Bikers push a hand lever to

Motorcycles can have different types of wheels and tires.

Some motorcycles have windshields that help keep bugs and dirt out of the rider's face

Brake lights and turn signals are on the back of the motorcycle.

operate the front brake. They push a foot lever to operate the rear brake. Brakes work by using friction. The brake pads rub against a rotating disc, or drum, fixed to a wheel. The clutch and shift let the motorcycle rider change gears.

Other controls on a motorcycle are the ignition switch, starter button, headlights, gauges, warning lights, horn, and speedometer.

Motorcycles also have mirrors. They allow riders to see what is behind them and beside them. A kickstand keeps the motorcycle standing up when it is not being used. Some motorcycles also have special features such as a radio or backrest. These features make motorcycle riding comfortable.

Most motorcycles have a kickstand to keep them from falling down.

The frame of a motorcycle is like a skeleton in your body. It holds the motorcycle together. Most frames are made of pressed steel. Others are made of aluminum alloy or chrome alloy. Aluminum alloy is much lighter, but just as strong, as steel.

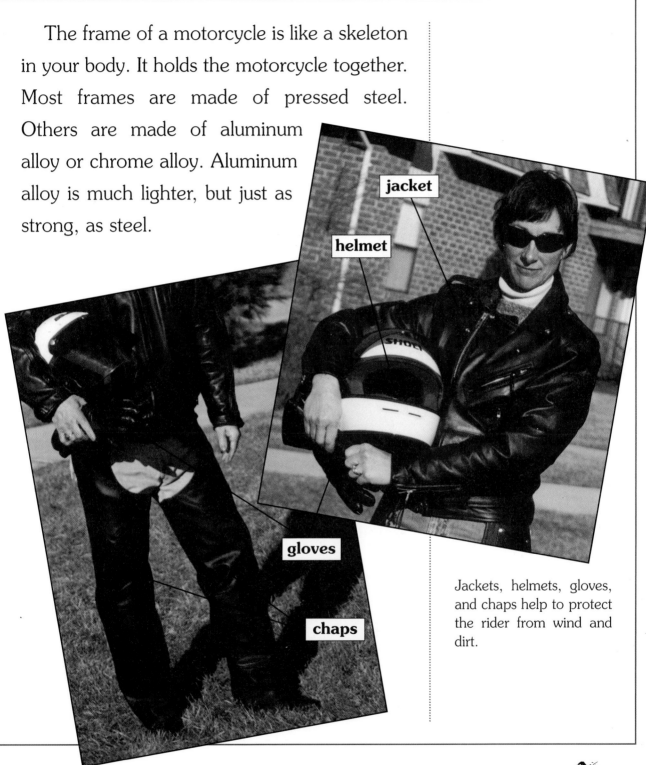

jacket

helmet

gloves

chaps

Jackets, helmets, gloves, and chaps help to protect the rider from wind and dirt.

Chapter 3

History of Motorcycles

In 1885, a German engineer named Gottlieb Daimler attached an engine to a wooden bicycle frame. This became the first motorcycle. Daimler became known as the father of the motorcycle. Other inventors experimented with different designs. In America, the first motorcycle was made in 1869. But motorcycles were not made in factories until many years later.

The first American company to make motorcycles was the Indian Company. It began making motorcycles in 1901. Two years later, William S. Harley and Arthur

Before motorcycles were invented, some people used bicycles to get around (left).

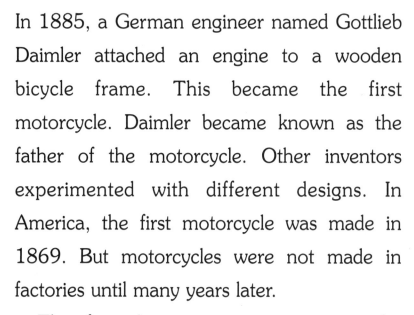

Davidson started making motorcycles. These first motorcycles were practical. They were faster than bicycles. They were an inexpensive way to get around. By 1909, Harley and Davidson began making motorcycles for sport. Motorcycle racing soon became very popular. Many cities built racing tracks called motordromes.

World War I began in 1914. The United States Army bought thousands of motorcycles. They were cheaper than other ways of getting from one place to another.

Motorcycles were very useful to the army because they were cheap and used less gasoline.

They also used less gas. Some of the motorcycles had sidecars. They carried machine guns and ammunition. Others carried stretchers with soldiers who had been hurt. When the war ended in 1918, many people continued to use motorcycles.

Racing became very popular. One race, the

People loved to watch early motorcycle races.

Enduro, began in 1917. The race is called Enduro because riders must have endurance, or the ability to keep going. Teams of riders compete. The race lasts for several days. The teams must cover hundreds of miles each day. They also must keep up a certain speed.

By the 1930s, speedway racing also became popular. But when World War II began in 1939, Americans stopped racing motorcycles. At home and at war, motorcycles were used as cheap transportation. After the war ended in 1945, soldiers formed

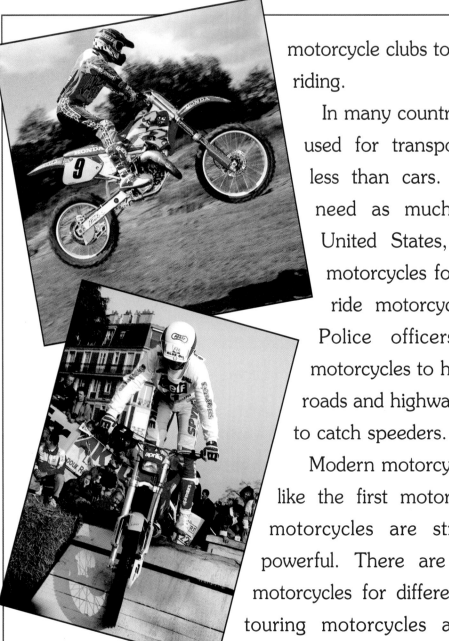

motorcycle clubs to spread their love of riding.

In many countries, motorcycles are used for transportation. They cost less than cars. Also, they do not need as much gas. But in the United States, most people ride motorcycles for fun. Some people ride motorcycles for work, too. Police officers sometimes ride motorcycles to help control crowded roads and highways. They can go fast to catch speeders.

Modern motorcycles look very much like the first motorcycles. But today's motorcycles are stronger, and more powerful. There are different types of motorcycles for different uses. Street and touring motorcycles are for roads and highways. Dirt bikes are for trails and racetracks.

By the 1980s, many companies in Japan

Motocross events let the rider do tricks and almost fly over bumps on the track.

were making motorcycles. Companies like Honda, Kawasaki, Suzuki, and Yamaha sell more than half of all motorcycles in the world.

People like motorcycles. In 2000, more than 19 million people rode on them. But as motorcycles became more and more popular, worries about safety also grew. Motorcyclists must share the road with vehicles much bigger than they are. And motorcycle riders are not as protected as drivers of other vehicles. Many states made laws making riders wear helmets. They made safety courses to teach riders how to safely use a motorcycle. Many states also make motorcyclists pass a special test and get a motorcycle operator's license.

This motorcycle can go fast!

Chapter 4

Why People Love Motorcycles

Many companies have made and sold motorcycles. But three companies stand out from the others. They are the Indian Company, Harley-Davidson, and Honda. These companies helped motorcycles become the popular vehicles they are today.

The Indian Company was the first American motorcycle company. George Hendee, a bicycle maker, met Oscar Hedstrom, a racer and inventor. They decided to team up and make motorcycles. They built a factory in Springfield, Massachusetts. In 1901, the first Indian motorcycles rolled out the door.

This is an early type of the motorcycle (left).

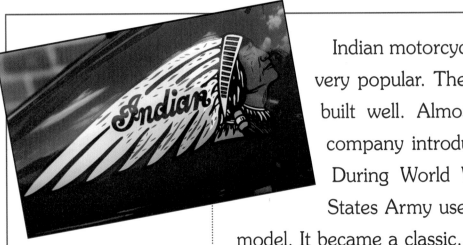

This is a logo on a motorcycle made by the Indian Company.

This is a 1941 Indian Scout.

Indian motorcycles quickly became very popular. The motorcycles were built well. Almost every year, the company introduced new features. During World War I, the United States Army used the Indian Scout model. It became a classic.

Another classic was the Indian Chief. It was designed by Charles Franklin. The model first came out in 1922. As the years passed, the design became more and more elegant.

This is a 1946 Indian Chief.

By 1948, the Chief had a fancy, fringed-leather saddle, chrome grab-rail, and chrome headlights. Fenders with skirts hid part of the wheels.

The Indian Company made excellent motorcycles. But after the Great Depression (1930s), the company began having money problems. Businessman E. Paul duPont bought the company and tried to help it. But it was too late. By 1953, Indian was out of business.

Market in Panic as Stocks Are Dumped in 12,894,600 Share Day; Bankers Halt It

The stockmarket crash in 1929 led to the Great Depression.

That same year, Harley-Davidson celebrated its 50th birthday. In 1903, William S. Harley and his friend Arthur Davidson built a motorcycle. They began to make them to sell. By 1907, they built a factory and made 150 motorcycles. The company was based in Milwaukee, Wisconsin.

In 1909, Harley-Davidson began making sport models. Arthur's brother, Walter, entered a race called the Long Island Reliability Run. He won with a perfect score. From that time on, Harleys competed in all types of races and sporting events.

Like the Indian Company, Harley-Davidson made motorcycles for the United States Army during World War I. By 1920, Harley-Davidson had become the biggest motorcycle maker in the world. Some classic models are the Sportster, the Easy Rider Chopper, and the Tour Glide.

Harley-Davidson had its ups and downs. But today, it is the only American company making motorcycles. On June 12, 1993, thousands of bikers went to Milwaukee to celebrate Harley-Davidson's 90th year in business. A parade featured 60,000 Harley-Davidson motorcycles.

The United States Army used motorcycles, like this one, during World War I and World War II.

This is a 1966 Honda police motorcycle.

Honda is the third motorcycle company that had a big effect. Soichiro Honda, a Japanese businessman, opened the Honda Motor Company in 1948. A year later, he began making motorcycles. In 1959, the first Honda motorcycle was sold in the United States. They became very popular.

Like Indian and Harley-Davidson, Honda makes good motorcycles. Honda's greatest effect was its message. In 1962, Honda began airing TV commercials. They showed people of all ages and sizes riding motorcycles. The theme was, "You meet the nicest people on a Honda." Before, many people thought they should not ride a motorcycle. Motorcycles were for other people. After the Honda commercials, sales soared. The CB750 was built in 1969. It was very fast. It could outrun any other motorcycle on the road.

Today, Harley-Davidson and Honda continue to make motorcycles. And the Indian Company is getting back into business.

This is a 1975 Honda.

This is a Honda GoldWing.

Chapter 5

Biking: Big Business

Millions of people love motorcycles. They buy at least one bike to race or ride. Some buy more than one! They wear clothes made especially for motorcycle riding. They take trips to watch motorcycle races. They buy souvenirs and collectibles. All this excitement creates thousands of jobs.

Each year, companies make more than two million motorcycles. Engineers are needed to design them. Sales

Many people enjoy riding motorcycles.

Motorcycle mechanics know how to fix engines and other problems.

people are needed to sell them. Mechanics are needed to repair them.

The Motorcycle Safety Foundation offers classes on motorcycle safety. So far, about two million people have taken the classes. Teachers are needed at places all over the United States. Some states require special permits to drive motorcycles. People are needed to give these tests and grade them.

Other jobs are for people who like to design and make clothes. Many motorcycle riders wear special clothing. Their jackets and pants are made of strong fabrics such as leather or Kevlar™. The clothes protect riders from falls, heat, cold, wind, or rain. Some clothing has bright neon stripes. The stripes make it easier for other drivers to see motorcyclists at night.

Riders also need helmets. A full-face helmet or a helmet with a face shield keeps dust and bugs out of the rider's eyes.

This biker looks like he is learning how to ride his motorcycle safely.

More important, a helmet protects a rider from a serious head injury in an accident.

Other necessary items are goggles, gloves, and boots. Goggles protect a rider's eyes. Gloves protect a rider's palms, knuckles, and fingers. Boots protect a rider's legs from engine burns. They also protect a rider from rocks and trash on the road. Many people

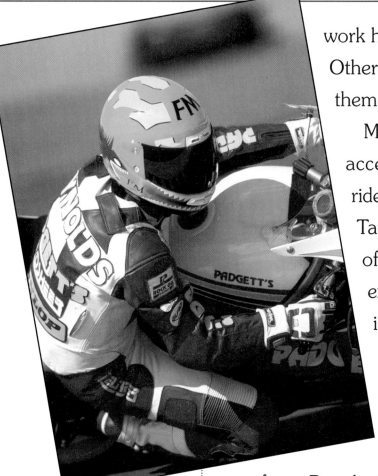

No matter what type of motorcycle, riders wear special clothing and helmets.

work hard to make all these items. Others work hard to advertise them, and to sell them.

Many bikers also buy accessories. Saddlebags give riders a place to put things. Tank bags are placed on top of the fuel tank. They offer extra storage. A clear pocket is on top of the tank bag. It helps the rider keep track of maps.

Every year, motorcycle races attract millions of fans. People travel from far away to see grand prix and motocross races. There also is the annual road race at the Daytona International Speedway in Florida. For one week in March, almost the entire city is involved with the racing event.

In every town hosting a race, hotel and restaurant workers take care of visitors. Other workers sell snacks and souvenirs to people.

Motorcycles also have made jobs for builders. Milwaukee is planning to build a huge building in honor of Harley-Davidson. Hundreds of people will be hired to build it. Hundreds of others will be hired to work there.

Motorcycle racing is very popular.

The Future of Motorcycles

Motorcycles cost less than cars and other vehicles. They use less gasoline. They are easier and cheaper to maintain. They do not pollute the air as much as cars. They do not need much space for parking or storage.

Motorcycles also can lead to lasting friendships. Motorcycle fans join clubs to talk about their vehicles. They take group trips. They enjoy being with others who share their love of this form of transportation.

One club is for people who like Harley-Davidson motorcycles. It is called Harley Owners Group, or HOG. A group member is

This man is trying out a new type of motorcycle (left).

Groups of motorcycle riders get together for many reasons. These riders are riding to help raise money for a charity.

called a "hog" member. Some people call their Harley-Davidson motorcycles "hogs."

At motorcycle rallies, bikers meet to enter races, perform stunts, and have fun. Rallies bring many riders and fans together. The American Motorcyclist Association has more than 235,000 members. It has about 1,200 clubs all over the United States.

People use motorcycles for work and pleasure. Police departments in many cities, counties, and states use motorcycles. They patrol highways, streets, and parks. College students ride motorcycles to classes. Some parents even run errands on motorcycles.

Even people who do not ride motorcycles enjoy watching others ride or race them. Whether zooming through mud and over bumps during a motocross, or zipping around the Daytona Speedway, motorcycle racing is exciting to watch.

Motorcycles look a lot like they did more than 100 years ago, when they were invented. But motorcycle makers are trying new materials. Some are using aluminum frames. They are lighter than steel frames. Carbon fiber is a new material. It is being used to make panels and gas tanks. Motorcycles of the future will be stronger and lighter. They also will be able to go even faster.

Motorcycles play an important part in the lives of many people. From the earliest days, they have been a popular way to get around. They could become even more popular in the future.

Police departments use motorcycles to patrol the roads and highways.

Timeline

1885—Gottlieb Daimler puts an engine on a wooden bicycle frame.

1901—Indian Company starts in the United States.

1903—William S. Harley and Arthur Davidson build a motorcycle.

1904—Harley-Davidson builds its first motorcycles to sell.

1917—Enduro racing begins.

1930s—Speedway racing becomes popular.

1949—Soichiro Honda designs new motorcycle.

1953—Indian goes out of business.

1998—Indian comes back as Indian Motorcycle Company.

Today—Motorcycles still are a popular way of getting around.

Words to Know

accessories—Added parts, items, or objects.

advantage—Something that is good.

alloy—A mixture of two or more metals.

cylinder—A tube that serves as the piston chamber of an engine.

maintenance—Keeping the motorcycle, or other vehicle, in good shape.

piston—A cylinder that fits closely inside a tube or hollow cylinder where it moves back and forth. The movement of the pistons in a car engine turns the car wheels.

pollution—The gases that are let off into the air from moving vehicles.

rev—To go faster.

sprocket—A tooth on a wheel that interlocks with a chain.

Learn More About
Motorcycles

Books

Graham, Ian. *Motorcycles*. Danbury, Conn.: Franklin Watts, Inc., 1998.

Hawkes, Nigel and Alex Pang and Chris Oxlade. *Cars, Trains, and Motorcycles*. Brookfield, Conn.: Millbrook Press, 2000.

Henshaw, Peter. *The Encyclopedia of Motorcycles*. New York, N.Y.: Chelsea House Publishers, 2000.

Ready, Dee. *Motorcycles*. Danbury, Conn.: Children's Press, 1998.

Learn More About
Motorcycles

Internet Addresses

Harley-Davidson History

<http://www.harley-davidson.com/CO/HIS/en/
history.asp>

*Tour a brief history of the Harley-Davidson motorcycle.
Lots of photos.*

Honda: Honda Racing

<http://www.hondaredriders.com>

Find out about different types of motorcycle racing.

Indian Motorcycle Company

<http://www.indianmotorcycle.com>

*Click on "The Company," then "Our History" to find a
timeline of Indian motorcycles.*

Index